Be One-of-a-Kind

Written by Beth Costanzo

Illustrated by Ekaterina Illina

The Adventures of Scuba Jack

BE ONE~
of·a-KIND

There are seven BILLION
people in this world.

But there is only **ONE** of you.

Accept your differences and be proud
of the way you are.
You are ONE-OF-A-KIND!

Everyone has something special to offer.
When you embrace your differences,
you shine and LIGHT UP the world!

Be bold and original!
Be different and weird.

Be dorky and creative.

Be nothing less than your awesome self.

FASHION

In a field of horses, be a UNICORN.

On a cloudy day be COLORFUL.

In a bowl full of bananas,
be a PINEAPPLE.

Use your uniqueness and strengths to better yourself and make the world a better place for everyone! Remember, you are an original. You are ONE-OF-A-KIND!

You were born to stand out and not blend into the crowd.
What if we all loved each other and our differences? Wouldn't the world be a better place?

Here are some ways to make the world a better place.
Let's clean up the oceans and make the sea creatures happy!

Let's help feed ALL
the children of the world.

Let's be kind to all animals. They have feelings too!

How would you make the world
a better place?

How Do You CELEBRATE you and your ONE~OF~A~KIND POWER & MAGIC?

It's simple. I'm going to be
A ONE-OF-A-KIND
the best version of me!

The Adventures

of

SCUBA JACK

www.ingramcontent.com/pod-product-compliance
Lightning Source LLC
Chambersburg PA
CBHW061959090426
42811CB00006B/991